BLESSED ARE YOU

BLESSED ARE YOU

Beatitudes for Modern Man

CHARLES MURPHY

HERDER AND HERDER

1971
HERDER AND HERDER NEW YORK
232 Madison Avenue, New York 10016

Contents

BLESSED ARE YOU

Introduction

1.

THE beatitudes are the epiphanies of joy—happiness of the highest kind. If they are about need and sorrow, hunger and thirst, war and persecution, they are also about consolation, the purity of the heart, peace and mercy, the kingdom of God.

Nor do the beatitudes promise only a far-away happiness —at the end of some rainbow, while for the present we are left standing in the mud of human pain and work.

It is time for us to throw over the notion that the good things of the Christian life are all to come later, and that all the bad things are to happen to us now. The promises of the beatitudes are not mere future comforts. Real joy is something that we must help fashion for ourselves, and the sooner we begin to labor at it—create it—the better.

Jesus gave us the beatitudes early in his ministry. They are an affirmation of the holiness and happiness of life by a man who later died for our sins. Yet never were they revoked or compromised; and we can only wonder, and be encouraged in our hope, that the Man of Sorrows was also the Man of Peace, that the Resurrected One spoke no bitterness or hate, but only Love.

But we put on a long face, and if catastrophe happens, we attribute it to God, and say that it was "God's will." Yet what kind of father is it who enjoys seeing his children sad? We who are the sons and daughters of God have shaped a dour and arbitrary Father—in our own image. He is a Father of stingy bounty, and yet Jesus, his Son, promised us an abundance of life. And slowly, only recently, we are beginning to take him at his word, believe him. It is a shock to find that God wants us to be happy—he has given us glad news, beatitudes—when all along we thought that the best and only way to be a Christian was either to withdraw from the world, or, if we had to live in it, to make sure that we settled in a nice vale of tears, right next to the valley of the shadows.

In the beatitudes Jesus has told us not so much how to bear up, struggle on, as how to live in the full measure of joy. They tell us that at the end of tears there is laughter, and that it is better to laugh than to weep—that the knowledge of consolation is better than the ignorance, and sometimes the egoistic pride, of suffering.

Yet for all this, the beatitudes are also words of paradox and contradiction. For some among us, they presage special charisms and gifts of the Spirit. For some, the beatitude of joy is in the dark night of hope—and for these, our brothers and sisters, who suffer persecution, and hunger

10

and thirst, there is only the consolation that they work in the cause of right, and shall one day see God.

Whatever the beatitudes are for each of us, they are—as we shall stress over and again—not mere generalities, but something that *each of us* is to give specific definition and meaning for our own life. For above all the present times have restored individual witness, the charism of the single Christian. We are no longer a vast mass of people all thinking and acting alike, until finally witness had become a stereotype, and charismatics were looked upon as fools, and even dangerous fanatics harmful to the harmony of the Church.

We have opened up to a new age, we have awakened to a new consciousness, a new urgency that each of us is an active part of the Church, a vital and alive individual. It is a time for seeking out joy, not tolerating it, or even fearing it. It is a time for boldly offering and taking love, rather than mystifying it—or fearing it. It is a time for trying to understand what pain is, and trying to overcome it, once and for all, in us and in everyone, rather than accepting it as a warning gift of a senile, old father.

So this book is about joy, about a new age—and in that sense it is also about discovery, illumination, awakening. Let us now consider for a moment longer just what this might mean.

2.

We know from history, our own lives, what we have read and can see around us, that words of the greatest force and originality can also be, from another point of view, the most tedious of clichés. Politics is a good example—its tired slogans are the dead bones of what once were living and urgent truths.

But some words, of whatever force and originality, seem never to be accepted, even from the beginning, and thus never have the chance of becoming mere clichés. Prophetic words are such an example.

Prophecies are not mere predictions. They speak to the present situation. The rallying cry of the French Revolution—"Liberty, Equality, Fraternity"—may have seemed evident and urgent enough to the peasants of France; but the words of the prophets seem almost to defy understanding. They are interpretative, paradoxical, contradict what the times ask, and make demands of us that we are not prepared to fill.

The words of Jesus Christ are, so to speak, both self-evident and prophetic, almost clichés and yet hard to understand. They had the strength to knock Paul to the ground the first time he heard them, yet it took Peter three times to comprehend their meaning.

Chesterton once observed, perhaps with mere words in mind, that he was a man who with the utmost daring discovered what had already been discovered many times before. For words, tokens of reality, have to be interiorized individually, by each of us, and so long as we accept stereotyped definitions of a word, that word will have no meaning for us.

Words have to be brooded on, argued over, rejected, and finally, if they are any good, understood and accepted. And it is joy to understand the words of a friend, of someone who loves us; and it is joy to be understood, have our words interiorized, by someone we love. This is the way it must be between Jesus and each of us. It is time that, with the utmost daring, we discover just what precisely it was that Jesus meant when he said what he did. We must listen closely, be alert, be ready to respond—and this is at least as difficult as passing through the eye of a needle—taking up the cliché and forging it into something that is true, having meaning, that defines *ourself;* making revelation into something more than a long-ago declaration about some faraway things.

Trying to understand, pondering, listening again, "wrestling with a problem"—and finally we "see the light," to make use of an old cliché. Each of us has had this kind of experience. It is a time when we transcend the ordinary and enter into a special world of clarity and insight. Perhaps for some of us, like Paul, only one such moment is sufficient to prod us on. But others of us need at least three chances before we begin to comprehend.

Those special moments of clarity and insight—a wit has said that the sanest moments in an actor's life are those

13

when during a siege of stage fright he realizes the inadequacy of what he is as an artist. But this is not the kind of introspective moment we mean—and in fact there is probably more to the actor, who does something, than to the wit, who does nothing.

Nor are we referring simply to studying long over a problem in mathematics and physics, and finally comprehending what a difficult formula means, and thus what the answer is and why.

Rather, we mean those times of greater and grander discovery, sudden and indisputably authentic, when we realize that what we are seeing or reading or hearing has a tremendous and decisive importance for us—even if, for someone else in the same circumstances, it has little or no meaning at all. It is a small but major moment, and in mysterious, unknowable ways it shapes our future.

C. S. Lewis has recounted one such moment in his life, describing a time when as a young man he was visiting a bookstore and happened to pick up the Everyman edition of a children's fable titled *Phantastes,* written by a nearly unknown writer by the name of George Macdonald. Lewis had previously picked up the volume and had rejected it on a number of other occasions. This time, however, he began to browse more attentively, and "in a few hours," he wrote, "I knew that I had crossed a great frontier. I had already been waist deep in Romanticism; and likely enough, at any moment, to flounder into its darker and more evil forms, slithering down the steep descent that leads from the love of strangeness to that of eccentricity and thence to that of perversity. Now *Phantastes* was romantic enough in all conscience; but there was a difference. Nothing was at that time further from my thoughts than Christianity and I therefore had no notion what this difference really was. I was only aware that if this new world was strange, it was also homely and humble; that if this was a dream, it was a dream in which one at least felt strangely vigilant; that the whole book had about it a sort of cool, morning innocence . . ."*

Lewis's retelling of the incident, despite whatever else he also tells us, states one main truth: he had crossed a "great frontier." This was an awakening. Paul had it once. Peter, living in the aid and comfort of the Spirit, experienced it in that moment called a lifetime.

Perhaps mystics have such awakenings, discoveries, constantly—or only once. The Chinese ancients used to speak of the *Tao,* the "Way"—the daily routine of giving oneself over to constant deepening of self and work, to minute perfectioning, to awakening to the infinite in the smallest thing and to everything.

The Christian tradition of the cloister and the religious life has also been given over to this same interiorization—to making oneself different and new, shade by shade, every day, changed and transformed by the grace of God within —by hearing him anew within one each day, and making

* C. S. Lewis (editor), *George Macdonald: An Anthology,* New York, 1947, pages 20–21.

15

the effort each day to hear and answer always in a new and better way. "It is *I*, Lord, your friend and servant."

Every day in the life of St. Francis of Assisi was new—he had no need to discover everything, for he had discovered the One.

Awakening in whatever form, and it has a thousand forms, can perhaps best be summarized in the words of no less a one than Karl Marx. "There are moments in life," he once wrote, while still a student, "that seem to mark the end of a certain period, but also clearly indicate a new direction. At such transitional points we feel compelled to examine past and present with the eagle eye of the mind in order to understand our real situation."

Jesus Christ spoke of himself as "the Way," and once chided his apostles: "Have you no perception? Are your minds closed? Have you eyes that do not see, ears that do not hear?" It was not until Jesus could no longer speak that they began to understand. Seeing him on the cross, their eyes opened.

Paul too, apostle of darkness and light, urged the Ephesians to "live like men who are at home in daylight . . . Try to find out what would please the Lord; take no part in the barren deeds of darkness, but show them up for what they are." (5, 8. 10–11)

This book, then, is about awakening, hearing, finding the Way—specifically, the way of beatitude and joy, which is the way of Christian life. For some of us who hear it, the Sermon on the Mount is filled merely with pious clichés, banal good thoughts, slogans, which some day we are going to take more seriously.

For Jesus, however, it was like any other day. When he saw the crowds he went up the hill. There he took his seat, and when his disciples had gathered round him he began to address them. And this is the teaching he gave.

When he saw the crowds he went up the hill. There he took his seat, and when his disciples had gathered round him he began to address them. And this is the teaching he gave:

"How blest are those who know their need of God; the kingdom of Heaven is theirs.

How blest are the sorrowful; they shall find consolation.

How blest are those of a gentle spirit; they shall have the earth for their possession.

How blest are those who hunger and thirst to see right prevail; they shall be satisfied.

How blest are those who show mercy; mercy shall be shown to them.

How blest are those whose hearts are pure; they shall see God.

How blest are the peacemakers; God shall call them his sons.

How blest are those who have suffered persecution for the cause of right; the kingdom of Heaven is theirs.

"How blest you are, when you suffer insults and persecution and every kind of calumny for my sake. Accept it with gladness and exultation, for you have a rich reward in heaven; in the same way they persecuted the prophets before you.

"You are salt to the world. And if the salt becomes tasteless, how is its saltness to be restored? It is now good for nothing but to be thrown away and trodden underfoot.

"You are light for all the world. A town that stands on a hill cannot be hidden. When a lamp is lit, it is not put under the meal-tub, but on the lamp-stand, where it gives light to everyone in the house. And you, like the lamp, must shed light among your fellows, so that, when they see the good you do, they may give praise to your Father in heaven."

From the Sermon on the Mount
The Gospel of St. Matthew 5, 1–16
THE NEW ENGLISH BIBLE

CHAPTER ONE

Those Who Need God

How blest are those who know their need of God;
the kingdom of Heaven is theirs.

EVERYTHING in the Gospel is about needing God. In fact, everything in Scripture is about how man needs God, and needs the special things of God which will make him more fully man, and lead him to God.

Genesis begins with man having everything, yet needing a woman. And God gave him Eve.

The people of Israel were the favorites of the Lord. They were poor, oppressed, despised, but God established a covenant with them, and sent them strong leaders, bread from heaven, a promised land. What they needed most, however, he would also send: a Saviour.

The parable of the prodigal son very simply reminds us of the great need a father has to give away his love to his son, regardless of the price.

Mary Magdalen, who gave away so much love for a price before she had met the Lord, had received none in return.

But on seeing Jesus she understood her need—what real love there was to give and receive.

Even the apostles, simple fishermen of Galilee, must have felt a need for something, been restless for something beyond the daily satisfaction of hauling in their nets and sorting their catch. What must they have thought about, day after day? The Gospel tells us that Jesus was walking by the Sea of Galilee when he saw two brothers, Simon called Peter and his brother Andrew, casting a net into the lake. Jesus called to them and said, "Come with me, and I will make you fishers of men."

"And at once," says Scripture, "they left their nets and followed him."

What does each of us *need*?

What does it gain a man, asked Jesus, if he has everything in the world and loses his soul?

Adam and Eve needed to taste the fruit of the forbidden tree. They needed to become like God; and afterwards, when they were driven out of the Garden, they needed to cover themselves with leaves and clothing. They needed to have more than enough—even having God to talk to, as they strolled through the Garden in the cool of the day.

The Israelites were poor and oppressed, and everything seemed always to go against them. What did they need? They were slaves, persecuted by the Pharaoh. Though the Lord gave them bread, passage through the Red Sea, and promises, there was still the need for something more. In their trial and tribulation, the people thought that they needed power for revenge, not mere milk and honey but a splendid kingdom as comfort and consolation.

"You are a hard-headed people," said the Lord. What they needed was to understand.

Finally the Lord was sent to them—a Saviour, and at the age of twelve he conversed with the men in the temple, and they did not understand.

Yet his parents too did not understand. His behavior was a mystery, and Jesus' explanation hardly made anything clearer. But though Israel was forgetful, Mary "treasured all these things in her heart."

When Jesus went through the countryside preaching, often he was not understood. Other times he was understood too well. Once a crowd threw him out of the village, and threatened him with stones and death at the brow of a hill.

The scribes and the Pharisees are portrayed in the Gospels as men who needed nothing, and understood everything. They ridiculed Jesus, and attempted to confound him.

Some of the people had not only hard heads, but hard hearts, and one day they dragged this Man to the top of a hill outside Jerusalem and killed him. What was their need?

Did Judas need his thirty pieces of silver?

Jesus died because he did so many things that he need not have done. He ate with tax collectors, with publicans and sinners. He offered them friendship and understanding. He tried to understand their loneliness, their small everyday needs, even if it be simply in the sharing of a meal and a little conversation. He had no need to worry about his reputation.

The miracles that Jesus worked were often to help those in great need. He cured lepers who needed health, blind men who needed sight, dead men who needed life. Yet his first miracle was nothing more than to help a wedding couple that needed wine to serve their guests.

He died on the cross because the sins and indifference of men needed to be propitiated, the hard-headed people redeemed. He needed to give himself in love because he had so much love to give.

After the resurrection, Thomas needed to put his fingers into the Lord's hands and side before he would believe. Yet Jesus showed his hands, and guided the apostle's fingers to the wound in his side. Lovingly, he guided the apostle to belief.

"How blest are those who know their need of God," Jesus had said, so long ago on a hilltop in Galilee. Now, in the room of the transfiguration, he would tell them how the kingdom of God would be theirs.

The important thing to remember is that we simply recognize our need for God. Each of us has a different kind of need, and each of us expresses that need in a different way.

We must remember too that we need others in almost anything that we do. At the most basic human level, the child needs his parents in order to grow. He is accepted into a human family and learns to love, play, cry, draw numbers.

He needs his parents almost totally, and the more they give themselves, the happier he is and the better he progresses in all ways towards maturity.

But parents also need their children, of course—to learn again what tenderness is, patience, the importance of discovering trifles, of deepening into a new kind of love that they had never known possible. The need of parents for their children is also in some ways total.

None of us can get along in life without the help of others. Our education, work, relaxation all count upon our relying on others to give what they have: knowledge and encouragement, a strong hand, companionship. We have to give in return, because we too are needed by others in a variety of ways.

Sometimes it is not always clear what a need is—whether the need is ours or another's, and what its nature is.

When the world responded to the victims of the great Peruvian earthquake, or to the plight of the Biafrans during their civil war, it was clear that there was a severe need for the simple, elementary things of life—food, clothing, medical aid.

In the problems of the Third World and the racial minorities, there are these same kinds of needs, usually just as apparent if they are not looked at through a film of indifference or hate. But there is something more here—the need includes but goes beyond mere physical giving. We are asked also to accept—to accept the poor and oppressed as equals, to accept them in love and friendship, to use our hand not only to give bread, but to clasp the hand of the other in a pact of brotherhood.

The poor and oppressed are all about us—but that does not mean that we modern men and women of the cities and suburbs should not in some ways be among the "poor and oppressed" as well. Not only, when we count our blessings, should we set aside a portion of them for those in need, but we should also have a very keen idea of what it means to be poor, oppressed, without hope or future. This kind of attitude is commonly known as being "poor in spirit."

In the first edition of the New English Bible, whose translation we have used, the first beatitude is rendered: "How blest are those who know that they are poor." In the second edition, however, the beatitude is changed to read: "who know their need of God"—and the translators acknowledge here what they call "a bold paraphrase."*

Literally, the Greek means "Blest are they who are poor in spirit." But this meant little in Greek, and could only be understood in its special Jewish context.

Luke reports Jesus as having said simply, "How blest are you who are in need; the kingdom of God is yours." (6, 20) This meant literally poor—and it must have sounded just as odd to Jesus' hearers as it may seem odd to us today. For riches, not poverty, show that a man has been blessed.

Yet in the Jewish context, "the poor" had become a kind of religious force who, as opposed to the rich and influen-

---

* See A. E. Harvey, *Companion to the New Testament* (The New English Bible), Oxford and Cambridge, 1970, page 28.

tial, could be sure that they would ultimately be rewarded and vindicated. Jesus in this beatitude is endorsing this tenacity. He is saying that the compromises and injustices into which men are inevitably led by wealth and power are incompatible with the integrity demanded by God.

But corresponding to the physical poverty of these Jews was their spirit of poverty. It was this spirit which was uppermost in Jesus' mind. There should be no bitterness in poverty, no resentment. Just as the rich should not become lost in their riches, so the poor should not become lost in their poverty.

What is more important than either poverty or wealth is the spirit, one's attitude. And it is not possible to have true poverty of spirit and yet be ostentatious in wealth, corruptible, or irresponsible, or greedy with money, placing it above all other things. Poverty of spirit demands more than occasional contrition that one has not quite regarded and used his money in the right way.

And what are riches? Why are they usually thought of as being infinitely vast, an immeasurable amount of money?

Riches are simply anything which make us think that we are self-sufficient. A poor man can feel rich "in spirit" just as his wealthy counterpart can feel poor in spirit. In spite or pride, he can declare that he needs no one, will accept help from no one, and will not offer his help to anyone either.

It was thus that this first beatitude has been more modernly translated by the phrase "who know their need of God." It is harder for a rich man, but it is hard for all.

27

Merely coming to the recognition of this need can be difficult. Money, after all, has become a routine thing. It may give us problems, we may not have enough money for this or that bill, take this or that trip, buy this or that book or present, but most people nowadays nonetheless handle money "like second nature." In some ways we may think about it often, in other ways not at all, but in any case it is "bad taste" to think of it in anyway beyond its utilitarian purpose.

God too has become "a routine thing." We may not love him to our full extent, but we "get by"—we do the usual obligations, make a few efforts on our own, but we have it all down pat, "like second nature." What is wrong is that we are "poor in God"—we haven't enough of him. We must become "poor in spirit" towards God also.

It is not at all easy for men to be "poor in spirit," to "know their need of God." Even the promise of the beatitude—that the kingdom of Heaven shall be theirs—is a little unreal, far-off. This is especially true for modern men of the cities and suburbs, for whom there is little actual poverty, and for whom there is already, in a sense, a kingdom on this earth.

If you have a comfortable place to live and sleep, enough money to get by on, entertainment now and then, friends for companionship, perhaps a family, and travel occasionally and "see the world," that pretty much amounts to your own little kingdom, a principality of the heart.

The more this little kingdom grows in riches, the more a

good time is had by all, the harder it is to think of that other kingdom "far off"—though it is also within us.

On the other hand, trouble and strife in the little principality of the heart can also cause us to forget about God and his promise of a richer life. Too much hard work, family problems, constant travelling—and we either forget, or grow to resent or hate God, whom we blame for our misfortunes.

Having a good time, enjoying oneself, is hardly antithetical to growing in love of God. God is the Father who seeks only our joy. Like the father in the parable of the Prodigal Son, he bears no resentment towards us if we forget him and his love for us, and go off and leave him. He loves us whether we love him or not—and he wants us to be filled with joy and happiness whether we love him or not. But like a father, too, he wants our love in return. In the parable, the other son stayed at home and worked on the farm. But God the Father sent his Son to seek out his other sons and bring them back to his embrace, and one day to the beatitude of heavenly vision. If the beatific vision in which we see God face to face is our full joy, it must also be true that there is joy in the Father as he looks upon us in return, his sons and daughters, who have come to share eternity with him, a life everlasting.

Job is the man who knew what range and flux there could be in the principality of the heart, the kingdom on earth that each man makes for himself, and must learn to share with others—and not set up against God.

He had a comfortable place to live and sleep, enough

money to get by on, entertainment now and then, friends for companionship, loved his family—a man who enjoyed life to the full and yet loved God, and did not forget him in his joy, but shared it with him in thanks and prayer and conversation.

God put him to the test. Fathers do not have to test their sons who love them, because love is something self-evident and shared. But the test of Job was a special gift, a charism —a trial of love. The principality of Job's heart was utterly destroyed, and Job was left without money, or place to put his head, or anyone to help him. Trouble and strife were all around him, he worked hard, his family deserted him— but he did not grow to resent or hate God. He did not blame his Father for his misfortunes.

The special charism that Job was given was to show his poverty of spirit, his need of God, in both wealth and poverty, in good times and in bad times, in the companion- ship of friends and family and in the dark hour when he was all alone.

For ourselves, we may have it either good or bad—be com- fortable or in trying circumstances, have many friends or very few. Whatever the case, whether we be rich or poor, Jesus tells us that we must be poor in spirit and know our need of God. This is a *beatitude.* There is room for joy in this need, just as in some way there is room for joy in our daily life. Job, the pious and wealthy patriarch of Uz, did not despair. There was an inner joy that did not flag down under any circumstances, favorable or adverse, but grew at all times. So it should be with us. Like Job, we too must say:

> *Naked I came from the womb,*
> *naked I shall return whence I came.*
> *The Lord gives and the Lord takes away;*
> *blessed be the name of the Lord.*
>
> (Job 1, 21)

CHAPTER TWO

The Sorrowful

How blest are the sorrowful;
the kingdom of God is theirs.

It is unfortunate that so much about religion seems to be shaded over in sorrow, almost in a kind of fatalism that things are bad now and should get worse, that the way to heaven is a cheerless and unhappy one.

None of us escapes suffering, of course, but all of us should try to escape it when it comes upon us. It may have an irrational cause, it may have just "happened," but somehow or other our life is now caught up in it, and it is for us to gather meaning out of it, and then overthrow it.

In this light, suffering can be a gift, a charism of the Spirit. It descends upon us, from however senseless a beginning, and in bearing it we are to find its meaning, and thereby escape it.

But there is also suffering that has no meaning, that is only a trial that we are patiently to endure. It is a suffering so deep that it will bring us no knowledge—where indeed knowledge has become something inconsequential. This is a time when the human spirit is tested to the bone, and our only consolation is that the Spirit will give us at least the strength not to break. But this is a rare and special charism of the Spirit. It is a fire which most of us are spared.

For most of us, suffering is of a different kind. It is sporadic, haphazard, unexpected—and we should keep it that way. The danger with many people who suffer is not that it will destroy them, but that they enjoy it—although in that sense, suffering has indeed succeeded in destroying something vital.

There is an old, cynical, but true observation of human psychology: "It is all right to suffer as long as someone is watching."

Then suffering has become a mystique, turned to its own end, and we are no longer wayfarers on a dark and strange road, but willful strays unwilling to rejoin into the mainstream of life. Our tears no longer burn, and instead of the gradual joy of consolation and understanding, there is only pride and self-pity.

Triumph over suffering is a profoundly Christian thing. Our Lord underwent the pain and suffering of a terrible death, but afterwards he was transfigured, and his apostles and friends, no longer full of grief, "were filled with awe and joy."

When our Lord healed the lame and sick, or raised the dead to life, in each case, after tears of suffering there were tears of joy.

Yet it is odd that somehow suffering is equated with being

serious, with taking no chances, with not straying from the mark; while a cheerful attitude seems to suggest lightness of purpose, almost an inability to comprehend what is at stake, a carefree unconcern over the gravity of the situation. In the mystique of suffering there is no room for knowledge through joy, through a profound and open encounter with others in the dynamics of day to day living.

"How can I describe the people of this generation?" asked Jesus. "What are they like? They are like children sitting in the market place and shouting at each other,

'We piped for you and you would not dance.'
'We wept and wailed, and you would not mourn.'

"For John the Baptist came neither eating bread nor drinking wine, and you say, 'He is possessed.' The Son of Man came eating and drinking, and you say, 'Look at him! a glutton and a drinker, a friend of tax collectors and children!' And yet God's wisdom is proved right by all who are her children." (Matthew 11, 16–19)

Jesus delighted in good conversation, in "eating and drinking," in the company of children. His encounter with the Samaritan woman at the well tells us something of his sense of humor. Never is he described as being morose, downcast, pessimistic. He looked upon the coming days of pain and suffering with horror and revulsion, and asked that the cup be removed from him.

"*Suffer* the little children to come to me," he said. He seems to have been talking to those who would rather be "serious" and straight-faced at all times. Yet Jesus was being neither casual nor diffident in saying that God's wisdom is proved right by all who are his children. The tears of a child are brief, and last only as long as the pain. It is natural for them to want to be joyful all of the time. An unhappy child is a tragic and unnatural thing—as tragic and unnatural as an unhappy Christian.

Perhaps it is in our attitude to children, our attitude *as* children, that we have given suffering, so to speak, such a good name, and joy such a bad one.

We fit ourselves into the role of God's children and immediately expect to be reprimanded and punished—even if we have done nothing. God the Father is so just that we must always be doing something wrong. Our slightest move irritates him. He watches us with horrible, spying consternation, and is swift to seek retribution for our every failure. The only way we can win his favor is to take his punishment and somehow make him think that we enjoy it.

In human parenthood this kind of situation leads to psychotic children, and deranged parents who are no longer fit to raise young lives for a realistic adjustment to the world about them.

What kind of father takes pleasure in seeing his children punished, deprived of a good time? Who is just before he is loving? Who would rather use his hand to slap his child than caress him? Who gives eye for an eye, a blow each time the rule is broken?

Even in an army barracks the situation is not so serious as this for each infraction of the rules; but in the militant suffering Church, which is not to be confused with the Church of joy and resurrection, the uniform is dirge gray, and defeat is the best kind of victory. Its terms, in peace and war, are unconditional unhappiness.

Yet this is the kind of father that God the Father has been made into—not a King of Peace but an Emperor of War; a General who passes constant muster on thousands upon thousands of weary, faceless troops. We have taken the prayer, "Your will be done," and changed it into an insult: "It was God's will."

Every time there is pain, suffering, death, catastrophe, we think of God as somehow benignly unmoved, "sending" it to us "for our good."

If children die, we say that "they were too good to live. God wanted them for himself."

This is nonsense. This whole kind of thinking is nonsense. God the Father wants nothing more than children to grow up in the affection of their parents; for parents to deepen and mellow in the love of their children.

He does not arbitrarily send us "lessons"—a burning home, the death of a beloved friend. Only once was it necessary for God to cause someone to suffer directly—when he sent his own Son to die upon a cross. In dying, the Son redeemed all men and pledged to them his Father's bounty of joy and love.

God does not send us pain and suffering, but grace and opportunities to grow in our love for him, in our love for our brothers and sisters, in our understanding and love of ourself. The ordeal of Job is not something that all of God's sons must one day undergo. We said earlier only that we must have Job's confidence in his Father's love, his tranquil peace and joy, "poverty of spirit," that are not dependent on external circumstances, but on love.

For us, God is more like the father in the parable of the Prodigal Son—he does not test us, we test him. He loves us beyond all endurance, and awaits our return—not that he will have the mere satisfaction of our contrition, but so that he can share his love with us.

Jesus did not talk much of suffering, except in the last days, when he spoke of his own impending suffering and death.

Mainly, suffering is something that belongs in the Old Testament—the long-suffering of the people of Israel, the plight of Job, the songs of the Psalmist. The old covenant was established with fire and lightening among a people outlawed and hunted in the desert. The new covenant was instituted at a love feast, a meal, an agape—for even as the passion of the Lord was about to begin, he gave them the means to overcome suffering and to share their love for one another in fellowship and reconciliation. The suffering would last only a little while, but the joy of Jesus' agape would last until the end of time.

Jesus had spent his entire life, in fact, fighting suffering. He cured the lame and the blind, the lepers; he raised Lazarus because the two sisters grieved. He ate with the poor and the tax gatherers, whom everyone despised, because by showing love and friendship for them he helped to ease their suffering, and give them joy. This was agape too.

It is striking, in fact, how often in the Gospels food and drink are associated with suffering and joy. Jesus' first miracle was to make water into wine so that the wedding feast could continue and everyone have a good time.

Once, after the apostles had been out on the sea all day fishing, they returned to find our Lord waiting for them on the shore, having prepared for them a meal of fish and honey over a small fire.

A large crowd one day came to hear him, and after a while grew hungry. Jesus took bread and fishes, and blessed them, and there was now enough to feed all of the thousands who sat in clusters around the hillside.

Yet there are moments which perhaps all of us experience—when food no longer tempts us, and when, though we have a thirst, there is nothing that will slake it. Our appetite dries up. We lose interest in eating.

It can be this way too with love. Something comes over us, we can hardly account for it. We feel that there is no more love in us to give, the inner wellspring is gone. There is no hate for the other, no dislike or revulsion—but the love is gone.

This is a special kind of suffering, and it is called *dryness*. At times like this, one sinks to the rock bottom of faith, and holds on, not in despair, but on the other hand seemingly against all hope.

But the time of dryness is also a very special and personal

moment in love. Somehow, though "there is no love," there is a clear and bare preoccupation with the God who is our Father. This is a long moment of introspection, when we find time to look back and see how we loved him in the past, where we have failed, the special occasions of joy. It is an encounter of the plainest sort, unadorned, raw, direct. How long it will last we can never tell, yet it prepares us for a new outpouring of love both from within ourselves and from God, whose love once again we shall feel in rich measure in our hearts.

Few men have understood dryness as well as George Macdonald. He had known its labyrinths and mysteries, its purifying and strengthening nature, how it synthesizes the stray ends of our love and helps us to resummon our love in an ever new and creative way, from out of a depth made deeper by having been shown up as shallow. The following are a few of Macdonald's meditations on dryness, and on the uses of dryness:

That man is perfect in faith who can come to God in the utter dearth of his feelings and desires, without a glow or an aspiration, with the weight of low thoughts, failures, neglects, and wandering forgetfulness, and say to Him, "Thou art my refuge."

And when he can no longer *feel* the truth, he shall not therefore die. He lives because God is true; and he is able to know that he lives because he knows, having once understood the word, that God is truth. He believes in the God of former vision, lives by that word therefore, when all is dark and there is no vision.

So long as we have nothing to say to God, nothing to do with Him, save in the sunshine of the mind when we feel Him near to us, we are poor creatures, willed upon, not willing . . . And how in such a condition do we generally act? Do we sit mourning over the loss of our feelings? or worse, make frantic efforts to rouse them?

God does not, by the instant gift of His Spirit, make us always feel right, desire good, love purity, aspire after Him and His Will. Therefore either He will not, or He cannot. If He will not, it must be because it would not be well to do so. If He cannot, then He would not if He could; else a better condition than God's is conceivable to the mind of God . . . The truth is this: He wants to make us in His own image, *choosing* the good, *refusing* the evil. How should He effect this if He were always moving us from within, as He does at divine intervals, towards the beauty of holiness? . . . For God made our individuality as well as, and a greater marvel than, our dependence; made our *apartness* from Himself, that freedom should bind us divinely dearer to Himself, with a new and inscrutable marvel of love; for the Godhead is still at the root, is the making of our individuality, and the freer the man, the stronger the bond that binds him to Him who made his freedom.

Troubled soul, thou art not bound to feel but thou art bound to arise. God loves thee whether thou feelest or not. Thou canst not love when thou wilt, but thou art bound to fight the hatred in thee to the last. Try not to feel good when thou art not good, but cry to Him who is good. He changes not because thou changest. Nay, He has an especial tenderness of love towards thee for that thou art in the dark and hast no light, and His heart is glad when thou dost arise and say, "I will go to my Father." . . . Fold the arms of thy faith, and wait in the quietness until light goes up in thy darkness. Fold the arms of thy Faith I say, but not of thy Action: bethink thee of something that thou oughtest to do, and go to do it, if it be but the sweeping of a room, or the preparing of a meal, or a visit to a friend. Heed not thy feelings: Do thy work.

The true man trusts in a strength which is not his, and which he does not feel, does not even always desire.*

* *George Macdonald: An Anthology,* pages 23, 32, 34, 35, 36, 65.

41

How blessed are those who suffer dryness, who suffer in any way, said Jesus. For in faith they know their need of God, even though in love they cannot feel this love or express it, or even any longer desire to express it. By and by, in faith, dryness itself will dry up—it will take years or days. But dryness is only opportunity, "biding time"—it is not something that we can ever become accustomed to, something to take up, as one can do with suffering, and wear it on one's sleeve. "*Wait* in the quietness," said George Macdonald, "until light goes up in thy darkness."

This waiting is something active—"Do thy work." Never in suffering must we mope, despair, be self-pitying. The Father is a Father of love, and the community of the Church is a brotherhood of love—and this love will support us and overwhelm us in the end. At the root of suffering is joy, beatitude, for suffering leads to a fullness of love, "a fullness beyond measure"—given to us by a Man who suffered for us beyond measure.

CHAPTER THREE

Those of a Gentle Spirit

How blest are those of a gentle spirit;
they shall have the earth for their possession.

THE last people whom we normally associate with possessiveness are the gentle. But Jesus has promised them the
earth.

The word "gentle" in our language has an interesting
history and use.

It derives from the Latin *gens,* or people, "that which belongs together by birth." Hence *genere*—to engender, to give
birth to new people who will increase the family.

Eventually the word came to stand for "gentry," people of
noble and high birth. New members of this class grew up
to become gentlemen and gentlewomen.

"A firm but gentle hand" and similar uses of the word
seem to imply something of this heritage—a benign "but
firm" attitude towards those of a lesser class—for example,
towards those who worked one's land. It was an attitude
adopted towards one's social inferiors, whom one was al-

ways expected to be courteous to, as suited a gentleman, but never too close or friendly.

Eventually the word "gentle" came to suggest weakness, however, and a pejorative effeminacy, as the plain people grew in number and the gentry gradually diminished in its power and influence. If a man had a "gentle nature," it was implied that he was fit only to wear fine clothes, and was unable to work with his hands for a living.

We do not normally associate the gentle with possessiveness or possessions. But for a long time, gentlemen and gentlewomen—the gentry—were associated with practically nothing else.

In the working classes, any show of gentleness was a sign of weakness—a lessening of manhood. Gentleness was a woman's trait. Unfortunately, this is still the case with many people. A father shall not be gentle with his son, not wear the "kid gloves" of the gentry. Hard facts of life must be faced up to early. There is no time for affection, "coddling," parents holding hands with their children. In school, children were to be strapped when they got out of line. It is no wonder that when these children grew up, they either hated God in whose name all this punishment was done, or feared him and servilely expected to please him only so long as they remained unhappy, and made other people unhappy as well.

Yet there has been, of course, a counter-tradition, a recognition that gentleness is nothing more than an "ordinary" human virtue, an attitude that one should naturally have towards one and all. The example of Sir Thomas More comes to mind here. He had a simple respect and kindness towards everyone, whether they be close members of his family (including his children), his servants, peers, enemies, king. He did not affect gentlemanliness, but embodied gentleness itself.

True gentleness extends even to animals. It is a recognition of their living worth.

Gentleness is a lack of aggressive ego, whether that ego wants to be recognized either in servility or superiority, in the hard facts of life or the disdainful admission that reality exists at all. But it is not thereby something bland. As the example of Sir Thomas More shows, it is simply the modest recognition of one's own worth, one's place in the larger scheme of things, and the acceptance of oneself with no desire either to inflate or deflate one's worth in the eyes of God, friends, and self.

If gentleness is an "ordinary" human virtue, by that we mean that it is something that should normally be expected of all. It makes no extraordinary demands upon us, and it brings peace and tranquillity.

This ordinary virtue, if universally practiced, would bring an end to all war, racism, and hate. It would put an end to boasting, greed, and pride.

How paradoxical it is that divided mankind—the *gens*—need only to be gentle (that derisive word) in order to begin to restore unity and peace throughout the world.

Aggressive people cannot possess the earth—they will only

destroy it. The earth can be inherited only by those who work to make it a better place. The gentle will "possess" the earth because only they can possess it—can love and nurture it—love and nurture and "own" anything, in fact, because in owning they give themselves.

When Jesus promised the gentle, the "lowly"—the word has the same meaning in Greek—that they would inherit the earth, he was also alluding to a special kind of earth, a special land—the promised land, the kingdom.

The rulers of the oppressed Jewish race were intent upon possessing the entire world, and eventually they were to succeed in conquering all of it, only to see it destroyed. Even Jerusalem would perish.

"But my kingdom is not of this world," said Jesus.

"Do not put your store in riches."

A contemporary poet has put it this way: "Don't own anything you wouldn't want to leave out in the rain."

The earth, the rain—these bear special consideration, especially in our modern time. For we have put our store in riches—in the riches of the earth, and we are destroying the earth. The pure rain of nature—it falls over a hillside gouged with mine shafts and oil pumps. There is a special relationship between gentleness and nature, but it is rare now for men even to have the opportunity to open themselves to the wide mysteries of the earth, its abundance, and learn to grow gentle in its hands.

Nor is this special relationship to be put down as "nature

mysticism"—a fanciful communing with nature that leads to visions of the primal garden, when man and woman were innocents, and all about was paradise.

It is not pantheism either. God is not Nature, and Nature is not God. We say all of this because on the one hand men have worked to ruin nature, and on the other hand have only begun to understand it. Philosophy and theology have practically ignored nature—left it to the admiration and enjoyment of simple people like St. Francis of Assisi, to poets and painters.

In the beginnings of human history, nature was full of dark powers, demons of thunder, capricious gods of rain and drought. By the time of the early Church, however, the gods had long been safely mythologized in the popular culture, and nature was accepted for what it was. The seasons had been subdued and were a regular part of daily life. The harvests of the land were blessed, and portions therefrom offered up in symbolic thanksgiving to the generous Lord.

Yet over the centuries the "dark side" of nature was gradually to reassert itself. The astrological heavens were given powers over men's lives. The primitive geography spoke of a vast, mysterious ocean that ended into some abrupt, sheer, terrifying waterfall into the void. Alchemical experiments, forerunners of science, seemed to vest the earth with innumerable secrets and magic forces. The earth was the center of the universe because earth was inhabited by men—but it became central only in an abstract and finally doctrinaire way. Nature became an imposing system, and new efforts to comprehend and theorize about it, based on early scientific observation, were condemned.

Eventually, of course, the views of natural science came to prevail—but though in some respects we have come to understand more about nature, we have hardly begun to accord it its due worth and true centrality in our lives.

From science we have derived two main things about nature. We have learned of its incredibly long and complex history, how it has evolved, why the earth is shaped as it is and is inhabited by the living things that it is inhabited by.

Technological science has also taught us how to use the riches of the earth to our benefit—but we have taken this valuable knowledge and used it to plunder the earth.

The old idea that man is the center of the universe, that man ruled the beasts and birds of the air and all the things of the earth, had gradually transformed into the notion that, with the mighty tool of science, man could now conquer and dominate the earth—destroy once and for all the dark powers, take away its last mysteries, be completely in charge.

The consequence has been that whole cities and countrysides have been turned into wastelands. Beauty in a city is now something to be searched out. The Affton River that Robert Burns so sweetly praised in his poem is a sewer now, poisoned by men in Glasgow being busy dominating nature. Oceans are stained in oil, a sunset is red with the fire of factory chimneys, and streaked dark with their smoke.

The men who dominate nature are not gentle—we have

forgotten how to be gentle in abundance, and much of the reason is because we live in cities stripped bare of nature—where the ground is hard, and the walls are steel and brick, and even plastic flowers are something of a treat.

One reason why men of the past were close to nature is because they worked with their hands, harvested their food, and with their hands offered a token of their food to God in thanksgiving. The food from the harvest was prepared for eating with the hands—thrashed, picked, washed, cut, baked.

But now even our food comes ready-made—pre-packed, in bags or boxes, and all we do is pour in a powder, or stir in water, or warm up for a few minutes what someone else —a factory—has already cooked.

We have lost so many ways of being what old-fashioned romantics used to call "at one with nature."

In recent years, of course, we have finally begun to look upon what we have done—we have looked out over the wasteland, what was once a garden, and have seen that it was not all entirely good. Nor is there any time to rest.

We have learned that man the dominator of nature must become man the pacifier of nature. Nature must become livable, and not be destroyed—tamed, but not ruthlessly conquered.

This new work of restoring nature is a work of joy—of beatitude. Learning again the mystery of a blade of grass, we become again gentle and humble. We will never learn all the mysteries of nature, because many of them are mysteries of the heart.

God has promised the gentle that they shall have the earth as their possession. It is a possession that they cannot meekly await, expect to happen all by itself. Rather, the gentle must go out and remake the earth, not cynically, but in wonder and with a profound respect.

The new earth will be sown not by the unworldly, nor pillaged by the anti-worldly, but lovingly tendered by those who are worldly in the true and best sense—those who with a gentle hand will nourish it in abundance, share it with all, accept it, work and play in it, in reverence and joy.

CHAPTER FOUR

The Seekers After Justice

How blest are those who hunger and thirst to see right prevail; they shall be satisfied.

SHOULD we take the words of our Lord literally—that the blessed are those who hunger and thirst to see right prevail? Would Marie Antoinette have offered cake to the poor and oppressed peasants of France if she had known the despair of privation? Would the rich man in the parable have offered anything besides crumbs to the beggar at the side of the table if he had ever once known the luxury of a single piece of bread?

Where there is no justice, often there is a vast hunger among the people—a real hunger, for just the basic needs of life. And of course, too, there is that other hunger—for those other basic needs of life, what the French peasants called "freedom, equality, fraternity."

This special beatitude can often be misunderstood. It does not mean that those who are "far away," in another land, another place, suffering hunger and thirst and awaiting justice, are the blessed—though indeed they may be blessed in the sight of God.

It means that we who are well-fed and have secured justice for ourselves must now take upon ourselves the hunger of those in need, the thirst for justice of those who are poor and oppressed. This is the cause of right to which Jesus referred. Only when justice for all, and food for all, is finally brought about will we, and can we, be satisfied.

Let us reflect for a moment on the example of two different but heroic men, whose only thing in common, besides a name, was their almost overwhelming concern for other people—St. Vincent de Paul, the bishop and saint, and Vincent van Gogh, a painter. These two men literally hungered and thirsted to see right prevail. If they were never satisfied in their work, it was only because there was still so much to be done. If there was so much to be done, and if there is still so much to be done, it is because they were not given much help from others—from us.

Their example is important because it is a reminder that we are their heirs, that they have left work for us to continue. They are not meant to be merely inspiring, but thorns in our side, goads to our conscience.

Both Vincents were born in poverty, of peasant families. The birthplace of Vincent de Paul was Pouy, near Dax in Gascony, in southwest France; the year was 1576. He was ordained to the priesthood at the age of twenty-four, but continued at the University of Toulouse for another four years to take the degree of Doctor of Theology.

It is likely that by this time Vincent had nearly outgrown his peasant ties, and like many young men of his time had, through the priesthood, entered into a more or less comfortable world of scholarship and ecclesiastical tenure. Yet he was now to take a journey that was to change his entire life. The scholarly young priest was captured at sea by pirates and sold as a slave in Africa.

This extraordinary event occurred as Vincent was returning to Toulouse aboard a small vessel that skirted the Mediterranean coast. The ship was set upon by Barbary pirates, who murdered several of the passengers and wounded others, including Vincent. Those who remained alive were put in chains, and the pirates then sailed for Africa, where at Tunis they sold their hostages as slaves at an auction.

Vincent was purchased by a fisherman, and then was sold again to an aged Moslem, a humane man who had spent fifty years in search of knowledge and wisdom. He soon grew fond of his slave, to whom he gave long lectures on alchemy and Mohammedanism, and promised to make him his heir if he would renounce Christianity and adopt the religion of Islam.

Vincent would not agree to the bargain, however, and upon the old man's death he became the property of a nephew, who sold him again to a renegade Christian, a man with three wives. Luckily for Vincent, one of the wives, a Turkish woman, on learning more about Christianity from this strange educated slave from Europe, began to chide her husband for abandoning his faith. The slave owner finally repented, and he and Vincent escaped from Africa across the Mediterranean in a small boat, landing near Marseilles in 1607.

The rest of Vincent's story is well known. Eventually he helped to found the Congregation of the Missions, and devoted himself to working with peasants, the needy sick, foundlings, the aged. At Marseilles, mindful of what he had seen of wretchedness on the Mediterranean in his youth, he opened a home to comfort the ex-slaves who formerly had pulled at the oars in the galleys. He visited the slums and the prisons, and constantly sought help from other religious and from the laity to help him in his work. He was a solitary sign of contradiction—a man who took literally the biblical injunction to be his brother's keeper—in the worldly society of seventeenth-century Paris.

By nature, he once wrote, "I have a peevish temperament and am subject to bursts of temper. Without the help of God I would have grown hard and repellent, rough and crabbed." But working with the poor, there was no time to be temperamental, to think about himself above all others. Mornings after Mass he would cast on his great cloak and shuffle off down some street of Paris on a mission of comfort. Working tirelessly in the cause of right, he had become tenderhearted to the point of looking on the troubles of all men as his own.

Vincent van Gogh was an entirely different kind of man —tenderhearted but temperamental with a strange fire of love; a man who had studied for the ministry, yet for whom there was more truth in a potato than in all of theology; a man devout almost to the point of being a laughingstock.

Vincent van Gogh was born in 1859 at Zundert, in the Netherlands, the oldest son of a minister in the Dutch church. Zundert was a village in the middle of a poor country worked by small farmers who were predominantly Roman Catholic. For a short while Vincent was enrolled in a public school, but his parents thought that he had become too rough through his contact with other boys and removed him to home, and engaged a governess to teach Vincent and his younger brother Theo, with whom he was very close.

Eventually Vincent worked intermittently as an art salesman and bookseller, and though he usually spent most of his free time in sketching and painting, he gradually came to think that what he wanted most to do was to preach the Gospel. He entered a Protestant seminary in Amsterdam, but was unable to cope with the scholarly demands that were made upon him in order to meet the requirements of a degree. He would punish himself for not advancing sufficiently —for example, by sleeping on the floor, but soon he realized that he would much rather be out doing something than spending his time in study. He resigned from the seminary and took an assignment as an evangelist in the Borinage, a mining district in the south of Belgium, and one of the poorest and most desperate regions in all of Europe.

During this time, Vincent gave Bible lessons, visited the sick, and in the evenings taught the children of the house where he boarded. He devoted himself thoroughly to his work, and in his usual way exaggerated enormously—he gave away his clothes and his bed to others whom he thought were more in need, and lived in a shack, sleeping on the floor. But his superiors considered him overzealous, and warned him about his activities. When his contract expired, it was not renewed. During this time, there was a terrible accident in one of the mines, and Vincent was deeply moved.

Yet Vincent stayed that winter in the Borinage, with no fixed employment, living on the little that his parents and brother could provide him. Finally, of course, he moved to Brussels and took up painting full time.

Vincent van Gogh is a rare example of a man on fire, an over-zealot, what the French call a *naïf*—too ardent and intense to give and take by halves. The saints are this way too; though Vincent had a more tragic end, for whatever reasons, for in 1890, while in a mental home, he committed suicide with a gun. Years earlier he had cut off his ear—because someone had asked.

Before Vincent went mad, he was extraordinarily sane— if seeing to the core of reality is a definition of being sane. He was possessed by this core of reality, and could hardly notice that others, who were less possessed, thought him to be "far-fetched," not in touch with reality, too eager to be human and Christian.

To have extreme purpose is not to be mad. Though disease later destroyed him, in his youth he had rationally listened to the words of the Lord, and had taken that Zealot literally:

56

"How blest are those who hunger and thirst to see right prevail; they shall be satisfied."

A contemporary of Vincent's during his tenure in the Borinage was M. Bonte, a pastor in the nearby village of Warquignies, who later wrote as follows of his former colleague in the mines:

"I should like to satisfy you as much as possible by putting together some reminiscences of Vincent van Gogh. In fact, I knew him some forty-five years ago in the Borinage, where he was an evangelist (not a pastor, as he had no theological degree). He worked at Wasmes about one year.

"He was the son of a Dutch minister. I remember well his arrival at Pâturages: he was a blond young man of medium stature and with a pleasant face; he was well dressed, had excellent manners, and showed in his personal appearance all the characteristics of Dutch cleanliness.

"He expressed himself in Dutch correctly, and was able to preach quite satisfactorily at the religious gatherings of the little Protestant group in Wasmes which they had entrusted to his care. Another community in Wasmes had a pastor. He worked near the edge of the forest, in the direction of Warquignies; he led divine service in a former dance hall.

"Our young man took lodgings in an old farm at Petit-Wasmes. The house was relatively pretty—it differed considerably from the dwellings in the neighborhood, where one saw only little miners' cottages.

57

"The family which had taken Vincent in had simple habits, and lived like working people.

"But our evangelist very soon showed toward his lodgings the peculiar feelings which dominated him; he considered the accommodations far too luxurious; it shocked his Christian humility, he could not bear being lodged comfortably, in a way so different from that of the miners. Therefore he left these people who had surrounded him with sympathy and went to live in a little hovel. There he was all alone; he had no furniture, and people said he slept crouched down in a corner of the hearth.

"Besides this, the clothes he wore outdoors revealed the originality of his aspirations; people saw him issue forth clad in an old soldier's tunic and a shabby cap, and he went about the village in this attire. The fine suits he had arrived in never reappeared; nor did he buy any new ones. It is true he had only a modest salary, but it was sufficient to permit him to dress in accordance with his social position. Why had the boy changed this way?

"Faced with the destitution he encountered on his visits, his pity had induced him to give away nearly all his clothes; his money had found its way into the hands of the poor, and one might say that he had kept nothing for himself. His religious sentiments were very ardent, and he wanted to obey the words of Jesus Christ to the letter.

"He felt obliged to imitate the early Christians, to sacrifice all he could live without, and he wanted to be even more

58

destitute than the majority of the miners to whom he preached the Gospel.

"I must also add that his Dutch cleanliness was singularly abandoned; soap was banished as a wicked luxury; and when our evangelist was not wholly covered with a layer of coal dust, his face was usually dirtier than that of the miners. Exterior details did not trouble him; he was absorbed in his ideal of self-denial, but for the rest he showed that his attitude was not the consequence of *laisser-aller* (letting himself go), but a consistent practicing of the ideas governing his conscience.

"He no longer felt any inducement to take care of his own well-being—his heart had been aroused by the sight of others' want.

"He preferred to go to the unfortunate, the wounded, the sick, and always stayed with them a long time; he was willing to make any sacrifice to relieve their sufferings.

"In addition, his profound sensitivity was not limited to the human race. Vincent van Gogh respected every creature's life, even of those most despised.

"A repulsive caterpillar did not provoke his disgust; it was a living creature, and as such, deserved protection.

"The family with whom he had boarded told me that every time he found a caterpillar on the ground in the garden, he carefully picked it up and took it to a tree. Apart from this trait, which perhaps will be considered insignificant or even foolish, I have retained the impression that

Vincent van Gogh was actuated by a high ideal: self-forget-fulness and devotion to all other beings was the guiding principle which he accepted wholeheartedly.

"It will not revile the memory of the man to confess that in my opinion he retained one weakness: he was an incorrigible smoker. At times I teased him about it; a loather of tobacco myself, I told him that he did wrong not to give it up, but he ignored me—painters cannot do without a little spot of shade in the picture.

"As far as his painting is concerned, I cannot speak as a connoisseur; besides, he was not taken seriously.

"He would squat in the mine fields and draw the women picking up pieces of coal and going away laden with heavy sacks.

"It was observed that he did not reproduce the pretty things to which we are wont to attribute beauty.

"He made some portraits of old women, but for the rest, nobody attached any importance to an activity that was considered a mere hobby.

"But it would seem that as an artist, also, our young man had a predilection for all that seemed miserable to him.

"These, sir, are a few reminiscences which my aged memory has tried to collect . . ."*

There have been many others who have been moved to devote their lives to "working in the cause of right"—Charles de Foucauld, Francis of Assisi, Damian who said that even

* *Vincent van Gogh: A Self-Portrait* (*Selected Letters Revealing His Life as a Painter*), edited by W. H. Auden, New York, 1961, pages 62–64.

lepers, social outcasts from ancient times, have the right to decent medical provision and to simple human dignity. More recently, there have been Albert Schweitzer, Mahatma Gandhi, and Martin Luther King. This is idealism in the best sense—a noble summons responded to with the work of one's own hands. It is this same kind of idealism that sends missionaries to work among the poor and needy both at home and abroad, that sends Vista and Peace Corps workers to teach illiterates how to read and write and grow their crops.

Jesus said that those in the cause of right shall be satisfied. Yet by its very nature this kind of work is almost never completed. Where there is poverty and illiteracy on one side, there is technological repression of the individual (and of the nature about us) on the other. Men and women work for inhuman wages, mothers cannot adequately feed their children, schools are poorly equipped and under-financed, war is declared and innocent civilians victimized, prisoners are mistreated, hospital patients are inadequately cared for, minorities lack equal rights and privileges, a child is brutally punished by a parent. All of these are examples of man's inhumanity to man, and they will be eradicated only if the so-called foolish extremes of the two Vincents and others like them are looked upon not as the far-fetchedness of a few, but as the concern and duty of all.

"Leave behind your wife and mother and follow me," said Jesus. All that he meant was that the love he proclaimed was the most important thing in the world, and could not be transgressed—that if ever it came to a choice, one should choose love of Jesus over all other things.

Working in the cause of right likewise does not require that we leave others behind us. First of all, we join with them. We become neither indifferent nor merely knowledge-able about problems of social injustice. We must actually feel and taste that hunger and thirst for right—give some of what we have so that others may eat, work with the oppressed and taste the sweat from our brow.

Complete victory may never come about—yet Jesus prom-ised satisfaction. There is satisfaction in the hunger and the thirst, in taking the first step, and each subsequent step. This is not the smug satisfaction that one is doing something. It is the deep sense of joy—the deep sense of beatitude—that work, however laborious, is being done; that suffering, how-ever little, is being alleviated; that freedom and justice in some small section of the world is slowly being accomplished for a needy few. It is the assurance, expressed in the march-ing song of the southern blacks in their quest for equal rights, that "we shall overcome"—that the hunger and thirst are good, because they are shared by all in a common fight against the forces of ignorance and hate. The satisfaction that Jesus promised is that which Martin Luther King spoke of the day before his death—that he had been to the top of the mountain, and had seen the promised land.

CHAPTER FIVE

Those Who Show Mercy

How blest are those who show mercy;
mercy shall be shown to them.

THERE is usually little said about the imagination, except in some areas of literature and philosophy. It is usually thought to be concerned mainly with art. "Other people" have imaginations. Usually they are a bit off-balance, perhaps rather reckless, and not to be trusted at the ordinary level of life.

In popular thinking, imagination is regarded as something having to do with being far-fetched, unable to make realistic judgments, unable even to appraise the situation correctly.

There is, of course, some "serious" thinking being done on the imagination—theoretically speaking, it is entirely respectable. But practically speaking it has little to do with the affairs of men and women.

But let us be altruistic and make a categorical statement: without imagination, the ordinary will always remain ordinary; the "far-fetched" will be like a beautiful, ungraspable dream; realism will be a heavy burden. And we use the word "imagination" in its ordinary, even pejorative sense—

that is, as an area of consciousness removed from the ordinary things of life. Man will destroy himself if he is not imaginative.

We are speaking, furthermore, not only of man "in general"—of the great discoveries and inventions, of the works of art of a few, of the imagination of an elite.

"It doesn't take much imagination to see this or that," is a popular saying. It is usually true.

It is no use railing about how passive, deactivated, one-dimensional our culture has become for so many people—how in daily life we use our imagination and creative incentive to a minimum. It is just a fact, and we ought to accept it, and try to do something about it, starting with ourselves.

"Give me a place to stand and I will move the world," said Archimedes.

The modern equivalent of this famous boast should be: √ "With imagination and courage, I can change the world." Beginning with your own world, of course, and with the help of others.

It doesn't take much imagination to see or do this or that, because most of the things we see or do are ordinary to the point of being repressive routine, stultifying and lethargizing—unimaginative.

Dull religious routine never requires much attentiveness, much creative response. The spiritual life cannot be lived in a pew, because the hard bench will soon become a soft bed. It takes imagination to get out and do something—and humility to come in to that pew now and again for solace and rejuvenation.

If you are content never to do anything on your own initiative, always to wait until you are prodded into making a move, then you do not need much imagination to get by, day after day, day by day, in one long day where one is the same as the next, the last the same as the first—and you are no different either.

The life of St. Thérèse of Lisieux on the surface seems serene and tranquil, but it took hard work of imagination to become a saint. It took imagination to see a daily chore— chore after chore—as a new challenge, a new way of transforming an ordinary event into something far-fetched—an act of love in God.

In his poem celebrating St. Alphonsus Rodriguez, Gerard Manley Hopkins speaks of those whose glorious exploits bring them honor and renown; even of martyrs, whose heroic deed is an ultimate, "far-fetched" threshold-crossing from one kind of reality to another. Yet Hopkins alludes also to "that war within." This is the war between imagination and routine, between service and slumber. While others crowded their careers in conquest,

> *there went*
> *Those years and years by of world without event*
> *That in Majorca Alfonso watched the door.*

All practice of virtue, of life in God, requires some imagination. It will not do simply to sit back and think that imagination can only be the spectacular province of a few artists and scientists. That anyway is a different kind of imagination—a special charism of the Spirit. All of us must use our imagination to the fullest, and in that regard our imaginative capacity and capabilities are endless.

It took some imagination on Jesus' part when he pronounced the fifth beatitude to his hearers on that little hill in Galilee. This was a bold act of confidence on his part.

"Show mercy, and you will receive mercy."

This seems like such an ordinary and bland precept, hardly far-fetched. But of all the beatitudes, it is the most difficult to achieve.

It takes some imagination to show mercy—not merely once in a while—to give crumbs from our table to the beggar who happens to show up at our door.

Rather it takes imagination to *be* merciful, all of the time —to seek out occasions of mercy, to take the initiative, be inventive and creative, not merely await the kingdom but work to bring it about.

The first thing that we have to do in our imaginative reworking of mercy is to get rid of the notion that it is very genteel, associated with going out one day a week from our comfortable homes and doing "charitable work"—the notion that it is somehow connected with alms-giving, but in any case *giving,* presumably from largesse. We have taken the words of Shakespeare and given them the wrong sense: "The quality of mercy is not strained" does not mean that we must not strain ourselves, but that true mercy does not recognize any limit, any strain—holds nothing back, and gives all.

Alms-giving, occasional charitable work are certainly all to the good—not merely "commendable" but real means whereby we can show our desire to help our fellow men— but mercy is something infinitely more. It is literally something infinitely more, for it has been given to us by Jesus, and been entrusted to us to show to each man in abundance.

In the Old Testament, mercy was something that had to be begged from God. In the New Testament it is given without having been even asked for. And the mercy of Jesus was not "genteel"—it was not given only to the poor and the weak, the lame, to outcasts, sinners, publicans. It was given to all of these, in its own right and as a sign, but Jesus did not merely "show" mercy—he *was* merciful, towards everyone whom he met who should receive it. In the last days especially, he was merciful towards those who would show him none. This is often the paradox of being merciful—the burden and test of mercy. For being merciful often involves our suffering. It may mean not only giving what we have, but giving ourselves.

It is not always easy to convince ourselves that we are not the merciful kind. Usually we like to think of ourselves as being rational, clear-headed, reasonable about matters. We like to think that people get their "just desserts," because that way everything evens out. A child, now and then, on the proper occasion, should be administered a judicious spanking, so that he will learn to keep in line. We may deny someone a trifling pleasure simply because there mustn't be too much pleasure—and "spoiling." We hold back the cudgel, but we do not fear to use the switch.

It does not take much imagination to see that this was hardly the attitude of Jesus. He raised his hand against no one. And he found ways, every day—in a vast desert land with few villages and a small, widespread population—to show what his mercy was.

The world is much bigger now—and yet we have not yet figured out what it means to show mercy, to be merciful. We look upon the example of Jesus with dried-up imaginations —with fear and caution, too—and are afraid to take the first bold steps of mercy, and prefer instead to tread the old familiar ground.

Jesus did not ever visit prisoners, at least it is not recorded that he did in the Gospels. It takes some imagination to think of ways in which the Christian mission of mercy can be carried into the jails. Mercy takes courage, too, not merely in the doing, but in forming one's convictions as well. It takes hope—as with prisoners, to have the courage and hope to think that they can be helped into becoming new—educated and converted to living and upholding the values and conventions that men live by. It takes determination to make this mercy more than a show of words. It takes the effort of long days. Mercy is not shown in the demeanor of your face, in a gesture of the hand—it is *done,* it is work. Mercy may mean helping to educate, giving counsel, merely spending time to talk and exchange views.

All of the down-and-outers in a society need the special
ministry of mercy—prisoners, alcoholics, addicts, the handi-
capped. This kind of mercy is often a life-time's work. It is a
service, and from day to day it needs to be strengthened and
restored in prayer and confidence that God's will is being
done—for it is God's will that mercy be shown to all, that in
the sharing of love men will one day all be equal in love,
and that there will be no longer any special ministries, any
"down-and-outers," but that all will be the same brothers in
Christ.

Yet in some way, perhaps nearly everyone whom we meet
has some special need for our mercy—our merciful, uncon-
descending, understanding response to their needs and cares.
Children, old people, a tired friend—they are each in a special way in need of our affection, understanding, counsel, or
consolation. We must be careful to recognize these needs—
and not be harsh, supercilious, or whatever.

The mercy that we will be shown will be the mercy that
we will have shared—the love that unites all of us as brothers
and sisters of one another and in Jesus Christ. It is the rest
after the long labor is done—the work of spreading love and
justice in the world, and suffering persecution in the cause of
right.

The mercy that we will be shown will be like a mystery
of beatitude flashing throughout our being. It will be like
that peaceful consolation that Peter experienced anew on
that last day of his life, hanging on a cross with his face to
the hot dust and his feet to the sky—the encounter once

again, the continuing and abiding encounter with the merciful love of the Lord, who has shared our oppression, trials, happy moments, all our life, and now at the end welcomes us—to an eternity of the new creation. We have been made new, and we have worked to make ourselves new.

The mercy that we will be shown will also be in the everyday things of our daily life—the kind expression of the other, the hand on our shoulder, the unexpected pleasures of a small gift or remembrance.

Not even in our wildest imagination can we ever experience anything comparable to the moment when we come together, two people, and share in a special giving and taking of love. If this love has been warmed with the fire of mercy it will have a special deep meaning for us that will glow in our heart long after the moment has gone. For merciful love is of a profoundly personal kind—it imitates the love of the Father and the Son. It seeks no reward except the happiness of the other. God so mercifully loved the world that he sent his Son to save and redeem it. When we show love we save and redeem a moment that could otherwise have been lost in hate, pain, forgetfulness.

We have been shown mercy in abundance. The mystery and wonder and joy is that we shall be shown it again and again, and never tire of it, and share it again and again with others, and finally forever.

70

CHAPTER SIX

The Pure

How blest are those whose hearts are pure;
they shall see God.

WE have alluded several times to "ordinary language." The words we use in everyday life are, after all, our definitions of reality. Wit, nuance, sarcasm—all of these things depend for their effectiveness on the base of ordinary language.

Purity is a word that comes out of ordinary language, but is not ordinarily used. One is ambivalent or altruistic about what it stands for. There is nothing wrong with purity, but it seems a little "square," despite all kinds of earnest justifications of it.

It is always going to be that way, in any language, at any time. Most of us are not tempted by the extremes against which purity stands, perhaps; but nonetheless purity does go somewhat against the grain—or at least the idea of it. Anyone who goes about saying that he is in favor of purity is in for a lot of wit, nuance, or sarcasm at his or her expense.

Purity is the quintessence of something. In this beatitude it is most probable that Jesus was referring to sexual purity. But there are other kinds of purity, of course, and among the Hebrews in particular there were rites of purity—before entering the temple, or for mothers of newborn children. There was even a feast of purification. The body was something to be kept clean and incorruptible, something not to be "defiled."

Even today, Orthodox Jewish women take ritual baths in order to make themselves "clean" before they give themselves to their husbands; and there are some foods that are not eaten because they are impure and make one unclean. To be impure or unclean is to be unfit for another.

When we were children, our first confrontation with purity was with "bad thoughts." There was still a Jansenist holdover which implied that our Lord's warning about looking at another with adulterous eyes somehow extended also to little children—somehow especially to little children, for whom "bad thoughts" were all there was. They were to take special care not to see, hear, speak, but especially not to imagine any evil.

But purity got its bad name long before we were children. A few centuries earlier, a group of thoroughly disgruntled English Christians decided that things had gone far enough, and that it was time to get back to the hard quintessence. Naturally they called themselves Puritans. But ordinary language being what it was, it was not long before the

Puritans—among whom there were a number of great and brave, and truly fearless Christians—decided that the main aspect of purity was its sexual one.

Puritan daughters were named Purity and Chastity, though there is also one recorded instance of a weary father naming one of his daughters One More Time, and yet another Faint Not. It is easy to understand why, all in all, Puritanism eventually died out.

Yet Puritanism had become a synonym for the repression of all bodily joy, of excessive strictness in manners of morals and religion. The word "puritanism" was absorbed into ordinary language, and "purity" was given a new, pejorative gradation of meaning.

Purity's bad name can be traced even farther back, however. Medieval tales of chivalry had made it such a ludicrously purposeless thing, an ivory- or castle-towered precept for knights and damsels, that it was only right that the greatest writer of his age, Miguel de Cervantes, took up the cudgel of ordinary language and knocked it down into something laughable but at least understandable.

But it makes no difference how far back we can trace purity's bad name. As we said before, it has always had a bad name, and it always will. Despite perversions to give it an excessively good name, as with the medievalists and Puritans, it still goes against the grain.

Because purity is a quintessence, it therefore suggests incorruptibility, and sound unity and wholeness of mind and body. It cannot therefore be something only partially attained.

Nor is it passive, resistful, defensive. It is bold and assertive in its pursuit of purpose and expression.

Of course, we have been speaking of purity thus far as though it were a thing apart, and not really as something integral to the person—providing a unity, wholeness to the man or woman. But there is no such thing as purity as such —it is not something to be "safeguarded." There are only pure persons, who make and keep themselves pure with ardent effort and purpose.

What is the purpose of being pure? What is the purpose of wholeness and oneness within oneself? How is a pure person "bold and assertive in his or her pursuit of purpose and expression"?

Because being pure implies wholeness, it has important psychological, physical, and spiritual aspects all of which are contingent on one another and are in constant dynamic interaction with one another.

A pure person is one who expresses love for another with his or her *whole* being, holding nothing back.

A married man or woman who loves his or her spouse with body only, and carries a secret hate or resentment, is cynical in love, and not pure, for he does not love wholly, with his entire self.

Likewise, one cannot love another merely with the mind only, and fear to express this love physically. This shows a false understanding of one's body, an incompletion, a non-wholeness—this imperfect love is impure because it is "too pure."

In a true, pure exchange of love there is no cynicism, no self-serving, a recognition of the entire reality of the other. It is an acceptance and giving of all of one's self and all of the other. The purpose of purity is the purpose of love, and the expression of purity is the expression of love.

Yet love, the foundation of our being, is a many-storeyed foundation. It is a complex thing, rare and unique to each person. And because expressions of love can be so varied and complex, because each of us can build on the foundation of love in a different way, it is obvious that love is many-charismed. Love is universal but not monolithic or uniform. There are different kinds.

A special kind of love is called virginal or celibate love, and for this kind of love there is a different kind of purity.

A celibate or virgin does not suppress his or her body and destroy the integral harmony of his or her being. There is a negative aspect in his love in that he foregoes the physical expression of it, but on the positive side he must, paradoxically, see this denial itself as a gift, an offering to Another and to others. If a celibate or virgin is only negative, isolates purity into something to be vigilantly "safeguarded" above all other considerations, then he or she has turned the idea of wholeness and integrity into a caricature. There is no longer a "whole" attitude to one's self, but a fear of one's

75

self—almost that kind of cynicism towards one's own body that a cynical married man or woman can develop towards the body of the spouse.

Virginal or celibate purity is not "more pure" than married purity—purity *per se* does not exist, first of all; it is something that a person is. A married person can be wholly pure, or fail in it, and a virgin or celibate can be wholly pure, or fail in it.

The celibate or virgin is asked charismatically to offer up the use of his or her body in the expression of love as a sign of love for God. It is a gift of self—but in giving to God, one must not take away from others. It is a special and difficult thing to offer one's body to God, it is a charism of an unusual and complex kind, and for that reason the pure celibate or virgin (this is somewhat redundant, but in that sense so is "pure married person") must take special care that this gift is in no way lessened. A *vow* of purity is too often regarded as sufficient, the *fait accompli.* All that remains is incidental.

Married persons too, though in a different sense, also take a vow to be pure towards one another. "With this body I thee worship," says the bride.

The celibate or virgin says the same to the Lord. The vow is only the beginning—the *fait,* so to speak. The accomplishment takes a lifetime, and a lifetime is made up of days—day after day of giving.

One of the dangers of living a pure life, however, is pride, an egoistic satisfaction that one has lived better than others. This kind of purity is self-seeking, and does not seek the other.

All of the beatitudes have, in fact, their opposite—instead of mercy, for example, there can be self-righteousness. This is not mere indifference—there is, in fact, a very keen attention to matters. What often goes wrong, or is in danger of going wrong, is that we gradually diminish in our interest in others, and take up the slack with an increased preoccupation with our selves.

So it was with the seven virgins of the parable—who were asked to wait for another, but grew tired, and thinking of themselves, fell asleep and missed the arrival of the bridegroom.

The other, the bridegroom, the beloved, arrives into our life all of the time. We do not wait by patiently forever. Jesus was *sent* to us, and he does not stand in the shadows. In marriage, two people *give* themselves to one another in love. In the religious life, there is also a *giving* between two persons. Even in the single life there is giving—for in no case, in any kind of life, can there be giving only between two and no more. The sharing of self must extend to everyone around us. There must be "no time" to think of ourselves, to seek not the other but the self. We see ourself best in the image of the other.

In this beatitude, Jesus promises the pure that they will see God—see him face to face as the other. They will see too the pure image of those others whom they have loved wholly, with all of their self, and whose love they accepted —wholly and humbly.

That is why purity knows not only no pride, but also no shame. It is a response of the heart. All that is most important is the pact of friendship or love—it is the consideration above all others.

If there is risk in being pure, in giving, it is the risk that accompanies all creative purpose. In love, the other is not simply sought out, met face to face, and then loved to the full. There are also trials and errors, false starts, hesitations, failures, ever new beginnings, ever new consummations.

Yet purity endures—it will never be "triumphant," but it will always last, for so long as men and women trust and share in their love for one another and in God, are open and not secret in their love, confide their doubts, and allow themselves both to reveal the love that is within themselves, and to seek the revelation of love in the other.

The promise of the beatitude is fulfilled in love's every moment. Love grows always in the sight of the other. If there are mysteries, there are no secrets.

What is important, in other words, is not to "stay pure," but to *see*—to see the other always before you, to see God always face to face. Death and corruption bring on darkness. The pure will see God because, above all other considerations, they have kept their gaze steady, even when they grew tired, even when now and then what they saw seemed

78

on the verge of being too familiar, lackluster, without sheen and brilliance.

Purity is the quality of everyday love, but it gives to love the qualities of permanence and strength, and makes love one day eternal.

CHAPTER SEVEN

The Peacemakers

How blest are the peacemakers;
God shall call them his sons.

"You must not think that I have come to bring peace to the earth," said Jesus. "I have not come to bring peace, but a sword. I have come to set a man against his father, a daughter against her mother, a young wife against her mother-in-law; and a man will find his enemies under his own roof." (Matthew 10, 34–36)

These words do not so easily contradict Jesus' summons to peacemaking as they may at first appear. Jesus is the Man of Peace. He spoke often of peace, and promised to send a Comforter, a Dove of Peace.

"Be at peace with one another," he said. (Mark 9, 50)

"Peace is my parting gift to you, my own peace, such as the world cannot give. Set your troubled hearts at rest, and banish your fears." (John 14, 27)

But the metaphor of the sword does suggest how divisive even good things can be. Christianity itself once divided the world, and was looked upon as a threat.

81

⌐ Love can give almost as much anguish as it can give joy.

Jesus promised us a kingdom where love and peace would reign; but it is a kingdom that we must establish ourselves, with our own love and peace. When Jesus spoke of the sword, he was foretelling the anguish as well as the joy. Before there is resurrection, there is death.

Before there is reconciliation, there is war. Factions must be brought into unity. Weapons will not be melted down into ploughshares until we take off the armor of distrust, greed, hate, envy, vengeance, and are willing to walk in the unadorned simplicity of love—nothing but love.

It is proverbially easy to be in favor of some few things— motherhood and apple pie, for example. It is not all that easy to be in favor of peace—or so, at least, it would appear.

There are different kinds of peace, for example. There is unconditional peace, and conditional peace. There is honorable and dishonorable peace, provisional peace and peace at any cost.

There are some who think that if peace is immediately and almost arbitrarily established for its own sake, then the deaths of many will have been in vain.

Many others say that peace is never an arbitrary but an absolute thing, is always justified for its own sake, and that if it is not established immediately, then the future deaths of all concerned will have been in vain.

It is difficult to refute the idea that the life of Jesus was lived in the example of non-violence and peace at all cost. Jesus did not fear to seek out his enemies and engage them in conversation, but never once did he call for their defeat by violence and arms.

He said that they who live by the sword shall die by the sword, and for that reason, when his enemies came to kill him, he asked Peter to sheathe his weapon and not resist the soldiers. As a sign of his abhorrence of bloodshed, he restored an ear to the soldier that had been struck by the disciple.

One of Jesus' first disciples after his resurrection was Paul, who had gone about the countryside "breathing murderous threats against the disciples of the Lord." (Acts 9, 1) Paul too, after his conversion, never once called for the defeat of the enemies of Jesus and his followers by violence and arms.

Yet, despite Jesus' example, and that of his apostles, and of the great age of non-resistant martyrdom that followed, the clear command to be peacemakers—"Be at peace with one another"—was gradually nuanced, weakened, interpreted to mean something slightly else.

Christians became accepted by the populace at large, became part of the people, and finally became rulers of the people. There was a more important mandate to spread than the message of love and peace, and that was to spread the temporal power of the Church. The Dark Ages are rightly named, because the Crusades mark the darkest hour of the Church—a time when it became, generally speaking, not Christianity but Christendom. The cross was given a handle and blade. The sword became the new symbol of the followers of Christ.

The words of Jesus, that he had come to bring not peace but the sword, were indeed forewarning and prophetical. The paradox was not only that his simple message would not be accepted by the world, but that it would eventually be refuted by his own as well.

In the Middle Ages the beginnings of a political theology were developed. These concerned themselves mainly with concepts of kingship, a just war, the sovereignty of nations. There was little concern given to individual witness. The Church had become universal, and it was the presence, power, and maintenance of the Church that was important above everything else. The Church had become a vast hierarchy where structure was important above all, and where the people occupied the bottom place.

It was not long before the Church that had been founded by the Man of Peace was given a military metaphor: the body militant, whose members were soldiers. Theology built up a fortress whose spires reached almost, but not quite, to heaven—but in any case, high enough so as not to see the blood and carnage of a "just war" raging below.

There were a lot of silly—and dangerous—things said by the leaders of the Church at this time—the qualification that one could not kill a knight on Sundays or during Lent, for example.

By the nineteenth century, the political metaphor seemed almost to have become reality, as many of the better known papal encyclicals were concerned mainly with politics and the preservation of the power of the Vatican State.

Yet the people by and large were earnest and wanted to work "in the cause of right." With clear conscience they counted themselves among the sons of God. They denounced extremists who went so far as to want to put heretics to the fire. On the other hand, they thought that the example of St. Francis of Assisi, who did not want to kill even a squirrel or a bird, was a bit unrealistic. He was one of God's "pets," so to speak, whom he kept from harm. We have spoken earlier about the dangers of so-called realism and seeming to be "far-fetched."

So instead of simple precepts there was enlightenment. A realistic people had to be cautious, interpretative—nothing was black and white, except for the division of the world into infidels and believers; and later between "the Church above" and the "world below."

Because the Church had diminished in, and had seemed even to suppress, individual witness, the Church now became ineffective throughout the world—that is, politically, as something "bigger than all of us," as something not really a *body* politic" but a political structure that belonged to another age.

Now and then there were holy men, of course, charismatics, who saw the need for reform, and surely there were many among the people who lived devout and faithful lives. But as a whole, the Church was too much a part of the times to bear witness against the evils of the times.

When men invented new and better tools of war, the Church was useless in preventing them from being put into effect; and often encouraged their use, even when it was a case of Christian fighting against Christian.

The theories of a just war and the sovereignty of nations had somehow made it more important what nationality you were, rather than even the fact that you might also happen to be a Christian.

Men also invented new tools for conquering the earth, and soon they began to plunder it, ravage it, and sent in their children to work in the dark tunnels to scoop out its riches; and the Church was useless in preventing all of this, and sometimes pronounced it good.

The Church, which was to be a sign of contradiction to the world, seemed to be a sign of contradiction to itself.

Of course, our depiction will seem to be one-sided, as it certainly is, because we have emphasized the failures of the Church at the expense of its many achievements.

But that is the way it ought to be. The Church need not be concerned with glory, recognition, congratulations. For above all it ought to be concerned with finding out its failures and setting things aright.

The Church will never recover the primitive form that it once had, in the beginning, nor should it ever attempt to find it and restore it. But it will always have the same message, word, sacrament to give anew, and make anew.

How all of this is to be done is not always clear; even in the early Church there was dissension over how things were to be done—but one thing is clear: it must at least happen in a different way from before. There have been too many failures. Even politically the Church has now been divested of power—and in this way it is indeed like it was in its first days, only now it must not lead the way to a dark age but to the light of peace and love.

As a consequence of its new position in the world, the Church has begun to discover—or sometimes rediscover—some important fundamentals, mandates, words, charisms.

One is that individual witness, as we have said, is one of the most vital things in its life—that room must be made for the witness of all, and of each.

The Church has sensed too that in the future its life and influence in the world will be very different from what it was in the past; and it has sensed also that it has no fore-knowledge of what this future will bring, except that it will not have power, but be powerless, at the hands of the world, and that sometimes it may suffer from this power.

Karl Rahner has written movingly of this future time, and we will now quote from him at length.

"Everywhere there will be diaspora," Rahner has said of this future time, "and the diaspora will be everywhere.

"The stage of human history will accommodate everyone, and each of us will have everyone as a neighbor, and what each of us does will have an effect on how all of the other people live. And *each* means each nation, civilization, historical reality, and, proportionately, individual . . .

"Christians in this future time will form only a relatively

small minority. They will not have any special historical domain of their own, but will live in the 'diaspora of the gentiles.'

"No longer will there be any 'Catholic nations,' that make men Christians prior to their own consent. Non-Christians and anti-Christians will have full and equal rights, and perhaps it will be they who will define the character of society; and perhaps they will even coalesce in powers and principalities as forerunners and manifestations of the anti-Christ.

"And when the time comes for the State, or the super-State, in the name of educational uniformity, to impose a single ideology on all, with all the means in its power, it will not be a Christian message that will be proclaimed.

"Christians will be the little flock of the Gospel—and perhaps they will be esteemed, and perhaps they will be persecuted. And perhaps they will bear witness to the holy message of their Lord in a clear and respected voice, or perhaps again only in an undertone, from heart to heart.

"They will be gathered around the altar, announcing the death of the Lord and entrusting their own darkness (a darkness which, in the super-State, no one will be spared) to the darkness of the death of their Lord.

"They will know that they are brothers and sisters, because there will be only a few of them—only a few who have staked their own hearts and life on Jesus the Christ. For there will certainly be no earthly advantage in being a Christian.

"They will faithfully and unconditionally preserve the

structure of their sacred, unworldly community of faith, hope, and love—the Church, as it is called, as Christ founded it. They may even work to preserve it with the very tools of technology.

"But nonetheless that Church will have been led by the Lord of history into a new epoch. It will be dependent in everything on faith, and on the holy power of the heart, for it will no longer be able to draw any strength at all, or very little, from what is purely institutional.

"In the future, the basis of all that is institutional will be men's own hearts. And they will feel themselves to be brothers and sisters because in the edifice of the Church each of them, whether in the servanthood of office, or whether not in office, will depend on every other; and those in office will reverently receive all obedience from the others as a wonderful, free, and loving gift.

"All dignity and office in the Church will carry no honor in the world's eyes, of course, have no significance in secular society. It will no longer be a profession in a social and secular sense.

"The Church will be a little flock of brothers and sisters of the same faith, the same hope, and the same love. It will not pride itself on this fact, nor think itself superior to earlier ages of the Church, but it will obediently and thankfully accept its own age as what is apportioned to it by its Lord and Spirit, and not merely as what has been forced on it by the wicked world."*

* *The Christian of the Future,* New York, 1967, pages 79–81.

89

This may well be what the future of the Church will be like, but whatever it will be, it will not be continuous with the past, but abruptly different.

It will be a time, as we have said, of individual witness above all.

In this future time we shall have to listen very closely to the words of the Lord. It will not be enough merely to bow our head as we sit in a pew.

"Be at peace with one another," Jesus said. Be at peace with people even if they are not in the same pew. "How blest are they who shall be peacemakers; they will be my sons and daughters."

What is a chief feature of individual witness is that it is *urgent*. The time is now. There are no committees to refer things to. Action will not be taken by someone higher up.

If you think that you can fully express your duty of charity towards others by merely feeling confidant that there are organizations for those in need, then you may indeed look upon charity only as a duty—as something so important that it can be carried out only "officially." And you may think that the work of making peace in the world can also be more effectively carried out by large groups, others, official organizations—and that it is sufficient for you only to feel some concern now and then, when you read about war deaths (which are so official), or look at pictures in the newspapers about blood and carnage that is being carried on somewhere—somewhere far away.

If you think in this manner, then you belong to the past, and the past is failure.

You are like the rich young man who was too filled up with comforts and satisfactions of doing nothing, filled only with good intentions. While there is holocaust around you, what good does it do for you to gain a peace based upon indifference and neglect?

CHAPTER EIGHT

Those Who Suffer Persecution

How blest are those who have suffered persecution for the cause of right; the kingdom of Heaven is theirs.

ABOUT all that seems to remain of persecution in modern times is the so-called "persecution complex." Persecution is something that people imagine is happening, but is not.

We know, for example, that there are desperately poor people in some parts of the country who are the victims of unjust laws, "dire" circumstances—but we know too that things are eventually getting better.

Persecution is when you want to destroy people—murder them, incapacitate them, render them helpless and harmless. But in modern times, in our neighborhood or world, there is only exploitation and neglect. Whatever else men today may do to one another, they certainly do not persecute in any systematic, large-scale way. Governments are spending money on education and housing for the oppressed and poor; committees are always at work studying nearly every aspect of their misery; and things are gradually getting better every day.

Even race relations have come a long way. There used to be race persecutions where entire populations were decimated. But now there are laws. Race persecution can land you in prison—if you are open about it.

Real persecution is when you want someone, some people, extinct. That kind of thing does not really happen any more.

And it is true, of course, that there are laws. In democratic life, there is no such thing as systematic, large-scale persecution. Laws, public opinion, the attained level of culture all prevent it from happening.

Perhaps we should therefore rephrase this beatitude into a form more widely suitable to modern times:

"How blest are those who have suffered *indifference* for the cause of right; the kingdom of heaven is theirs."

It would be easy to blame ourselves for a little bit of indifference. If persecution is not a widespread phenomena, at least indifference is. We can all identify with it. It can explain almost anything. We even get a bad conscience out of it—as on those times when we look at the photographs of human misery in the daily newspaper. We feel compassion, but never the urge to help resist some kind of persecution.

But perhaps history has failed on such a large scale that we can only think of persecution on a large scale. Of, most recently, the Nazis persecuting the Jews; or farther back in the Judeo-Christian past, the Romans against the Christians, or the Egyptians against the people of Yahweh.

Yet even if this kind of thing has not happened "in a democracy," it will not do to change the beatitude to read "indifference" instead of "persecution." All we have demo-cratically succeeded in doing is reducing persecution to a more personal level. Each of us persecutes, each of us can be persecuted. It is only by a common effort that persecution of any kind, large or small, will be eliminated from the face of the earth.

In any way that you contribute to the needless unhappi-ness of another man, you are persecuting him.

In any way—if you ignore him or abandon him, like that traveller who passed by the man on the road, and left him to the Samaritan. This was not a case of mere indifference. It was condemning him to pain and death.

If you think that it is enough merely to think about the poor and the oppressed, and develop a sweet kinship of com-passion, and not do anything to help them, then you have done nothing to relieve them of their pain. You persecute them *with your indifference*.

And it is not only the poor and oppressed who are perse-cuted by all of us, each of us, every day, in our active neglect. Those whom we love we also persecute, now and then, when the fancy strikes us. Each of us knows in an instant how this is so.

Jesus talks about *suffering* persecution, however. It is im-plied in his words that we should not persecute others; but it is explicitly declared that they are blessed who suffer in the cause of right.

Persecutions have been the occasions for numerous martyrs and heroes to rise up in heroic opposition. Even democracies

have martyrs and heroes. Why? Because democracies are
founded in the cause of right—and right must be achieved
with sweat and tears of all the people, in laws, constitutions,
amendments, referendums, vetoes, enactments, editorials,
manifestoes, debates, free speech, votes, confrontations, sit-
ins, marches, lobbies, committees, assemblies, juries, mora-
toriums, bread lines, and everything else that it takes slowly
to move a people forward.

All of this takes suffering. To be an active part of the
people working for right means suffering persecution—
doing something in the cause of right.

No matter what you do, there will be someone to fight you
every inch of the way, and to find ways of persecuting you
into submission and defeat.

Twice in the beatitudes Jesus spoke of working in the
cause of right—twice he promised that our labor would
bring joy, to ourselves and upon the earth. Workers in the
cause of right must hunger and thirst for it, and be willing
to undergo even persecution in its cause, yet they shall be
satisfied, the kingdom of Heaven is theirs.

Perhaps Jesus stressed working in the cause of right because justice affects not only individuals, but all men in a
mutual way—not only those who have been set upon un-
justly, but those who are themselves unjust. Social attitudes
are so ingrained in us both as individuals and as a people
that even rethinking our prejudices or indifferences to the
plight of others cannot be done in some solitary way, but
must be worked out almost piecemeal, step by step, with

others. The work of righting social wrong is so vast that it almost demands that individuals join together and create justice and equality and brotherhood for all by their mutual effort. Individual witness, the personal seeking out of one to another, is still vital—but it must be part of a common cause. When Jesus sent out his apostles to preach the message of love, it was clear that his followers were to set up communities, that people were to bind together and build upon one another's mutual labor. There was much room for personal action, but there was too much to be done for there to be any solitary laborers in the vineyard. The harvest is always urgent, imminent, and of great proportion.

Today there are many ways in which men and women can join together in the mutual cause of social right—these extend from the neighborhood to the national level, and beyond that to the international level in the United Nations, which was established, in the words of Pope John XXIII, "to protect effectively the rights of man, rights which are universal, inviolable, and inalienable because they are based directly on the dignity of the human person." (*Pacem in Terris,* article 4)

If neighborhood, city, national, or international organizations fail, that is no reason summarily to dismiss them as ineffective. They are only as strong as the individuals working within them. The satisfaction must come not from "I told you so" but in "We must try again to do what must be done."

One of the most important areas in the cause for social

right—even on the international level, but most importantly on a local and personal level—is education. Emerson, speaking with the nineteenth century's confidence in progress, called education the best tool of the masses. It may be that, but the situation is more complex.

Education is not a mere boot-strap. Democracy is not filled with all kinds of ladders and ropes leading down into the pits where dwell the poor and oppressed—who need only laboriously to climb up and take their position with others as equals.

Those who are "more equal" than others who are only theoretically equal must stretch out a helping hand—go down into the depths of persecution and help the suffering slowly climb out of their oppression. Or to use another image: the walls of ignorance and injustice must not be climbed over—they must be destroyed, by those on either side, working together.

If you have something that you can give to another—if you can teach him, help him learn—and thereby assist him in throwing off his burden, then you are working in the cause of right. A group of such teachers are a community in the cause of right—a mutual recognition of wrongs, solidarity in making right.

Carrying out the "works of mercy"—that is, simply being actively merciful in a Christian way—can also be important work in the cause of right. Bringing food or medical aid, and companionship, helps destroy the injustices of hunger and disease, and loneliness.

Beyond physical injustices, there are those, less tangible perhaps, but as oppressive or more, which are caused by hatred, prejudice, the obsessive pursuit of power. Here there is a lack of recognition that an individual is an individual, that he or she has any worth at all, any dignity— thinks and feels like a real person, and is in fact the same as any other human being. It is the attitude that one may have towards animals—they are all alike, none different, none deserving of any rights—subservient above all else. It is a blind, repugnant refusal to see and admit that in the sight of God, men are equal; and that in each other's sight, all men must accord equal rights to all others, act as an equal and expect others to act as an equal.

Simone Weil called equality "a vital need of the human soul." She said that equality consists "in a recognition, at once public, general, effective, and genuinely expressed in institutions and customs, that the same amount of respect and consideration is due to every human being because this respect is due to the human being as such and is not a matter of degree."*

The first step in recognizing others as equals is in recognizing ourselves as being no more than equal. It is seeing ourselves as "a human being" and not as a super-being, a special being set above others, apart from others. This is a great joy—a beatitude—that discovery of oneself as what one is, nothing more and nothing less. It is a discovery that we may perhaps have to make many times over, but there

* *The Need for Roots*, Boston, 1952, page 16.

must be a first time—and it is one of the most important moments of our life.

The discovery of others, all others as individuals, are also important moments, and are constantly being made again and again. There is a nearly infinite number of such discoveries possible—because each person we meet we have to see as unique and different from all the rest. The discovery does not just come upon us. Sometimes it takes work—and there are times for each of us when we seem to be challenged to the utmost. But it may be just that person whom we are having difficulty with that we must not abandon on the road to some Samaritan. The most arduous discovery can be the most rewarding, for both you and for the other.

For in all cases, the other has the right to be recognized, discovered. Whatever the circumstances, we must first see him as another man or woman, a human being in the same way that we are a human being. This recognition is a gift of self because we are holding nothing back, we have voyaged forth—perhaps across a universe of a few feet—to clasp a hand in friendship and brotherhood. We have announced our willingness and readiness to be at some kind of service to the other—in simple companionship, in a mutual effort to relieve him from some form of suffering or oppression, in the sharing of some pleasure, or whatever.

Persecution will one day die out only when there are no more persecutors—when all have shown their solidarity in a common willingness to undergo risks and share in oppression until it has been utterly overcome.

Right and equality will one day come for all when we have all learned the joy—the beatitude—of a simple truth. We are, each of us, all of us, no more than human beings— and when we have understood what it means to be a human being, a being with feelings, dreams, aspirations, vulnerability.

This joy will come, finally, in the knowledge and comfort that a Man came among us, came to each of us as an individual, and gave us a love that makes us nothing less than human beings—that makes true brotherhood not only possible, but something that can be lasting. It is a love that, if we make it our own—and that means if we share it with others—can help us to overcome all obstacles—the obstacle of self, the obstacle of the other.

In the kingdom of justice that man must build, is now building, there will be no fences, no defenses, no offenses. It will not be a paradise, but at least there will be joy. There will be no rest, but the work will fill us with a humble satisfaction. And the serpent of hatred and prejudice shall have been thrown out of the gate, and banished forever.

101

Accept It with Gladness and Exultation

1.

NOWHERE in the beatitudes is there any mention of love. Yet Jesus, who spoke them, is the Man of Love. It is something taken for granted—taken almost heroically for granted. Love is where all life is grounded, tested, transcended, made worth living.

Are the beatitudes a "summary of the Christian life," as they have been called? The Christian life cannot be summarized. It cannot be catalogued or defined. It can only be attempted, failed, attempted again, and finally, with the help of others in the Church, and with the aid and comfort of the Spirit, in some way peculiar to each of us lived and achieved.

Yet there is one great beatitude from which all the others draw their strength, and if it does not summarize the Christian life, it at least succinctly states the message that we have received, are to make our own in our lives, and hand on to others: "Love the Lord your God with all your heart, with all your soul, with all your mind, and with all your strength. Love your neighbor as yourself." (Mark 12, 30–31)

103

In the beginning of this book we spoke about special moments when we cross boundaries of consciousness. But a person who locks himself up in a dark room will never see light. The doors of perception, as William Blake called them, will not open unless we take the handle and open them ourselves. "I am the door," said Jesus. (John 10, 7)

We said too that words are our definitions of reality—but so much depends on how we speak. Shorn of nuance, inflection, passion, sarcasm, warmth—whatever, a word is practically meaningless. It is the bare ground on which we build, either apart or with others, sturdily or badly. One of the cornerstone words is *love,* and how we use that word, what we mean by it, tells much about how well or poorly we have constructed our life—how much we think it is worth living, or not worth living.

Can love be defined—need love be defined? Anatole France used to say that people in love never bother about talking about it, much less trying to put it into the cage of definition. He suggests further that mere words so poorly convey what lovers want to convey that they never or rarely tell their love with a mere statement—"I love you."

It is interesting that nowhere in the New Testament does Jesus plainly speak of his love for another. John says simply that "he loved Martha and Mary," and all of the evangelists make it clear that the Father and the Son loved the world and all men without exception. But nowhere does Jesus *say* that he loves someone—rather he asks and urges again and again that he *be* loved, that his hearers love one another,

104

show their love with deeds stronger and bolder than mere speech.

For the love of Jesus could not be contained in a word, or in a universe of words—and surely the volumes that John speaks of at the end of his Gospel, which would be needed to describe all that Jesus did and which even the whole world could not contain, would be volumes about his love, huge and clumsy attempts to catalogue and define and express it.

Jesus *did* love, he *was* love—he expressed his love with what he did from day to day—and especially on the last day, for he had said that the greatest love of all was to lay down one's life for another.

In some ways, Jesus' words—and the word of his life—are so strong, forceful, without need of comment, that they seem hardly to require the usual appurtenances of language—nuance, inflection, passion—whatever. The word is spoken plainly and boldly, and we are asked to hear and make our response—give it our own context in our own life.

We are liars—we lie with mere words—if we say that we love God but do not love our neighbor—and this means that we are liars too if we only say that we love our neighbors, but make no effort to show it, enrich it, be willing to receive it in return. All words can be empty lies—the proof of truth, the joy of real definition, comes in active, individual initiative, witness, moving forth to another and to all others.

Paul was a man who seemed almost possessed by the

105

power and mystery of love. He spoke of it often, of its force in his own life, and how it was so vital that all the Christians be "brothers of one another" in love if the early Church was to hold together in the last age of suffering and persecution.

Just as Jesus gave his beatitudes early in his ministry, as a kind of foretelling affirmation of how he would live his own life and witness to its truth, so too Paul in one of his first letters gives his own beatitudes—affirmations of a new kind of love that he would bear out to the end, during persecution and imprisonment, and finally to death. They are a bold challenge to us still:

"Love is patient," Paul wrote to the Corinthians. "Love is kind and envies no one. Love is never boastful, nor conceited, nor rude; never selfish, not quick to take offense. Love keeps no score of wrongs; does not gloat over other men's sins, but delights in the truth. There is nothing that love cannot face; there is no limit to its faith, its hope, and its endurance.

"Love will never come to an end. Are there prophets? their work will be over. Are there tongues of ecstasy? they will cease. Is there knowledge? it will vanish away; for our knowledge and our prophecy alike are partial, and the partial vanishes when wholeness comes. When I was a child, my speech, my outlook, and my thoughts were childish. When I grew up, I had finished with childish things. Now we see only puzzling reflections in a mirror, but then we shall see face to face. My knowledge now is partial; then it will be whole, like God's knowledge of me. In a word, there are three things that last for ever: faith, hope, and love; but the greatest of them all is love." (1 Corinthians 13, 4–13)

Love will never come to an end, but as we grow from children to mature adults it grows to a wholeness. It is all things, and it makes us entire. The "reward" of those who love is love itself. "Blessed are they who love, for they shall be loved in return." Love is a beatitude because it is a joy. It is patient and endures, and there is nothing that it cannot face. The Christian is not one who is simply, magically "filled with love" for God and man. He or she must work at this love, create it, build it up—and this is done by seeking out the thou, the other, in each and every man and woman. For in Christ, as Paul said, we are all brothers and sisters, and there is no division any longer between us.

Paul was obsessed with giving himself, because he *was* love—a man of love, and he was obsessed with giving love. Like the "two Vincents," or Charles de Foucauld, the Curé of Ars, Francis of Assisi, he took the words of our Lord literally, even though in the eyes of the world he may have looked a bit unrealistic. "You must be fools for Christ," Paul had warned the Corinthians.

Love is not something that can be held back—not reserved, withheld, put off to another time, made exception to. The person next to you and the person across a continent, people whom you know well and people whom you have yet to meet, need your love, and you need to give it to them in turn. Deny this love and you are not only "a liar," you have deprived your life and the lives of others with joy, fullness, "beatitude."

A sour face, a spiteful distrust, any kind of prejudice, any laziness or indifference when others are in need, any shunned opportunity simply to be "kind" or to "envy no one"—these are the things from which discord and hate are born and nourished. For as we give love and receive it in return, so are we alone responsible for giving hate, discord, violence, nourishing these things, preventing the reign of love in the world. Love will never reign in the world until it first reigns in ourselves.

2.

The Sermon on the Mount was the occasion of Jesus' first teaching. In the beatitudes he both affirmed a number of traditional precepts, and offered paradoxical and unheard-of demands to a new and different way of life. The hill on which he spoke the beatitudes was most likely a lonely foothill in the northwest of Galilee. Matthew reports that Jesus spoke only after the apostles had gathered around him, but presumably too "the crowd" also had gathered and heard his words.

It should be clear, of course, that Jesus was not trying to divide men into "eight different kinds," or into the have's and the have-not's. The summons to a radically new way of life—one that contradicted the old way, and offered happiness not in the material things of the world, but in the riches of the spirit—was given to all men alike. Each man was to learn his need of God, be of a gentle spirit, suffer persecution in the cause of right.

The beatitudes were also spoken in the future tense, and referred several times to the kingdom of the life hereafter. Jesus meant thereby that his listeners should not expect immediate reward for their labors—that sharing in work and love were important above all other considerations.

Accept all of this with gladness and exultation, said Jesus. This was a bold and strange language: that insults and persecution and "every kind of calumny" were to be suffered with a sense of joy, even of exultation.

You are the salt of the world. The metaphor has several connotations—a few grains sprinkled throughout can change and enhance the flavor of a meal. Salt is a preservative. Jesus is speaking here especially to his apostles, to those who believe in him, and not to the unconverted. Each of them is like a grain of salt, and must adhere to the love which he has given them so as to keep it fresh and vital. They must spread out over the countryside, over the world even, making the old into new—making agape out of the simple elements of a meal.

You are light for all the world. Isaiah had said that Israel was to be "a light to the nations" (49, 6), and the symbol of this destiny was Jerusalem, set on a hill. But now there was a new light, not set up upon a hill to be gazed at from afar, but a light that would pervade and conquer the darkness of men's hearts.

After listening to the beatitudes, the disciples set forth again in the company of Jesus. As on that much later day on the road to Emmaus, they talked of many things. For three years they shared their daily lives with Jesus—argued with him, failed him, pleased him, rejoiced with him, finally suffered with him—and then suddenly they seemed to be alone. When Jesus returned to their company three days after his death, they were filled with awe and joy—beatitude. It was but the beginning of that same beatitude he had told them about on a foothill in Galilee at the start of his teaching. They had tasted now and then of this joy in the past, but now they were to taste of its fullness. They were to go out of the room and into the streets telling the people of a new kind of love—not only telling, but loving the people with a new kind of love.

So it is with us, with all who hear the words of the Lord. Love is our word, and alleluja our song. Together we must set forth, and find the New Jerusalem. There we will know beatitude in its fullness, but we will have known much of it too along the winding road of our life. Along the way, we shall have astounded both others and ourselves, converted them—and ourselves, with a new kind of love. "I am the Way," said Jesus. It is a way of ever new and deep discovery, advanced in humble love, sign-posted in the clear direction of an everlasting joy.